Hold On

WARNING

Do **not** look inside
Do **not** ask
Do **not** listen

Do **not** worry
Do **not** speak
Do **not** question

Do **not** turn this page
Do **not** think
Do **not** refuse

Do **not** do
    nothing
Do **not** do this

Pleased to meet you Mr Lear Jim Dalziel

HOLD ON

JAMIE INGLIS

© PROHIBITED PUBLICATIONS
MMVIII

Hold On
© Jamie Inglis 2000. All rights reserved.
Second Edition 2008
ISBN 978-0-9556810-2-8

The right of Jamie Inglis to be identified as the author of this work has been asserted by him in accordance with the Copyright, Designs and Patents Act, 1998.

Contact the author
info@jamieinglis.com

Many thanks to **Jim Dalziel** for kind permission to reproduce the *'Milestone Icon'* on the front cover, *'Serious Birthday Card'* on the rear cover and *'Pleased to meet you Mr Lear'* facing the title page.
jimprdl@blueyonder.co.uk

All photographs and other images © Jamie Inglis 2008.

Burning the Page - Internet Services
www.burningthepage.com

The Poetry Index
www.poetry-index.com

The Disorganised Society
www.disorganised.org

Printed by Lulu
www.lulu.com/content/1238907

Published by
PROHIBITED PUBLICATIONS
79 Bruntsfield Place
Edinburgh
EH10 4HG
Scotland
www.prohibitedpublications.com

By the same author

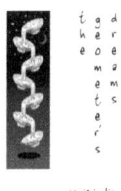 *the geometer's dreams*

 *fractals & mnemonics*

 *hold on*

 *gluon notes*

HOLD ON

previously

The Geometer and the Chinese Box	1
Mockquake	2
Choosing a Tattoo on the Train to Bergerac	3
Pinball Graveyard	4
Empty Cardboard Box	5

Operation Market-Garden

Operation Market-Garden	11
Landing at DZ-X	13
Walking the Lion Route	15
Here to remember	16
The Airborne Cemetery	17
Another cemetery for tears	20

more from Albania

For Mijellin	25
Martyrs of 39	26

some earlier

One hand speaking	31
Finding a church at home	32
The Matter Gap	33
Voting with their feet	34

Bloody Balkans

Small States Again 37
Defending our chickens 39
Goradze 40
World War CCC 41
Macedonia is a country again 42

Yesterday, Today and Tomorrow

Barrings goes down 45
For Bao Ninh 47
AKA The Chief Executive from Hell 48
Amsterdam coffee shop 49
That old refrain 50
Maybe Einstein was wrong 51
Tattoo Times 53
After the plague 54
Holding Patterns 55
A Good Netizen? 57
Courier 58

more new neologisms

gigadark 61
datadust 63
chaolist 65
chaologist 67
anti-org 69
gigaecho 71

Colophon

This is my art 75

previously

THE CHINESE BOX AND THE GEOMETER

Looking for prying eyes.
Hidden from all, but secrets.
Looking at life

Mockquake

Every year
when they practice
the Mockquake in Tokyo
it rocks the world.

The six wise men
of seismological science
announce abnormal data.
So take to the land.

The pulse to the city
starts out to sea
and takes nine seconds
to reach the superstructures.

Where tremors fracture
gas, glass and bodies.
Silence from Tokyo
shakes the world.

Choosing a Tattoo on the Train to Bergerac

What best suits you
from the catalogue in view.
As the train rattles through,
which one to pursue.

The strangers are gaping
as they see you in the making.
A multitude of signals,
yours for the taking.

Something small and simple
to hide that hated pimple,
or complement that dimple.
Perhaps a rose, on a pink nipple.

A Gothic patch to cover your back
but don't want to look like a motorcycle hack.
You're name, of course, for when I get back.
Where to place, that's the right track.

Pinball Graveyard

Where do all the old machines go?
When the electromagnets weaken,
the flippers begin to stick,
and the silver ball looses its shine.

Where do all the old machines go?
When the lights fail to flash,
the bumpers fail to bounce,
and the tilt is no longer a tremble.

Where do all the old machines go?
When the specials always light,
the excitement begins to fade,
and everyone scores the replay.

Empty Cardboard Box

I do not waste my dreams on sleep
I dream my dreams by day.

Living these dreams
I am just unable to lock away.

I do not dream of islands
but follow the flow by day.

Living these dreams
in the harsh light of play.

I do not dream of flying
nothing clouds my dreams by day.

Living this dream
of finding somewhere to stay.

Operation Market-Garden

There are some places you visit
where the ghosts are very vocal

Operation Market-Garden

Operation Market-Garden
the idea was unstoppable.
Again that old military lie
'We'll all be home for Christmas'.

04.11.96

Monday

Arnhem on Wednesday

Landing at DZ-X

Landing at DZ-X
that quiet Sunday afternoon
of September seventeen.
Time enough to make char.

Only ten sticks of men on the lion route
will reach the north end of John Frostburg.
This day.

Walking the Lion Route

Walking the lion route in the pouring rain.
Down from the airborne cemetery into Oosterbeek
two field hospitals stand exposed at the crossroads.
Back to headquarters at the Hartenstein
the airborne memorial a spike in the gloom.
Down to church that will be the escape
and set out on the lion route, the low road to town.
First the railway bridge blown in our faces.
Then Nelson Mandelaburg new to the town
a quiet shelter from the torrential rain.
Halfway to the bridge, stop at the promenade.
On in the rain, a downpour to believe.
A final rest under the ramparts.
Then the stairs up to the ramp
and a moment or two standing in silence.
Here to remember
and for a moment the sun shines.

Here to remember

I am of the next generation
to follow after these brave men.
It is our deathly obligation
to visit after these brave men
and follow their steps until they fell.
To listen to the stories of these brave men
telling of their comrades never going home.
To remember here these brave men
and see again their bloody, needless, end.

The Airborne Cemetery

The airborne cemetery,
the only one in the world.
For men with wings
who dropped from the sky
over Arnhem that fateful day.

An airborne cemetery,
for those seventeen hundred men.
Who will forever rest here
in a field near Oosterbeek
after dropping in battle in the days to come.

11.11.96

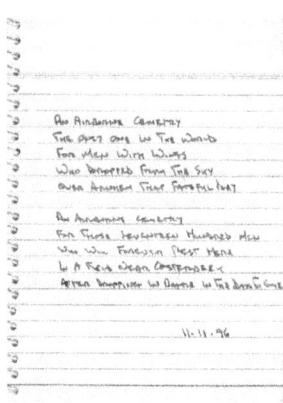

Another cemetery for tears

Another cemetery for tears
far too many over the years.
What happened, to all our fears?

Another cemetery for tears
more soldiers forever held dear.
Resting in a field forever near.

Another cemetery for tears
white crosses and neat rows here.
Always the price is way too dear.

Their Name Liveth For Evermore

more from Albania

For Mijellin

When I listen, all I hear
are the songs of the heart, of poverty and sadness.
And when I look, all I see
are signs of the mind, painful to see.

What do I know of this world here
so distant from mine.
My life feels so out of time
that I must retreat to my dream.

Why, when I ask, is this so strange
the answers come tumbling but senseless.
For here this is real, if only tonight,
and tomorrow, we shall all wake to this.

Martyrs of 39

The memorial to the martyrs of 39
has faded now, and the glass is all gone.
Pillboxes fill the tranquil gardens,
where old men sit, playing chess
and reminiscing of these bright days.

Before the photos were removed,
and the martyrs became faceless.
Now their glory and their grace is gone,
the garden to weeds and war preparations.
Their fight is a long time over,
and the next already begun.
These brave martyrs, soon dust and gone.

some earlier

One hand speaking

Speaking with one hand
The scratch of pen on paper
Speaking through the air
To those who will listen

Speaking with one hand
Attempting to scratch the pain
Of speaking to you out there
Hoping that someone will listen

Speaking with one hand
Scratching down another page
Nearly finished speaking now
Is anyone still listening?

Finding a church at home

As soon as I walked through the door
I knew it was a religious service,
such things are ever the same.
Recognisable in every life
as a hushed contemplative awe
in silent cloistered worship sites.

And when the door crashed closed behind me
and I twisted to confront this traitorous noise
and twisted back to the eyes of the congregation
and stood as close as I could to a faint
and then waited for the service to end.

**The Matter Gap
(No More Big Bang)**

Late piece of the jigsaw doesn't fit
Last few pieces forced into the wrong hole
This is the end of the beginning
Started 15,000 million years ago
At 10^{-35} seconds
Storm in a cosmological tea cup
The galaxies showed red shift and
    were deemed to be expanding and departing
    by Hubble
    in 1939

Penzius and Wilson heard the radio echo
    of that first bang
    in 1965

More than enough to keep on expanding
We are at the critical mass density
Ten times more matter than we have found
Where is all this cold dark matter

Then come the stick men and galactic holes
Large scale structures of clustered galaxies

Too many large structures
For cold dark matter prediction
So no more Big Bang

**Voting with their feet
(the refugees of circumstances)**

The exodus of the century closes the millennium.
Everywhere, refugees mass in great numbers
crushing against the borders of state and mind.
Pressing the boundaries, desperate,
numbing pain and belief, contorting the truth,
of a shimmering safety mirage, uselessly apparent
at the end of a conviction that help is near.

Only the refugees of precarious circumstances,
forced to depart the peril of a nation's situation
disturbing the ability to stay and survive.
This tortuous displacement of surviving life.
Voting with their feet,
the refugees of circumstances.

Bloody Balkans

Small States Again

Returning to the time of small states.
When there was Thrace
at war with Macedonia.
And the world was tribes again
disputing over ground,
that was rightfully theirs,
since the time of there forebears.

And the small state comes again.
Our civilisation is ending,
as so many others have before this,
by descending into anarchy.
Small states again.

Defending our chickens

Getting worse in Sarajevo town
as the convoys stop
and night falls.

Shells in the night
gunfire in the night
tracers in the air.

Illuminating our huddles
lit by candlelight
and never silent.

Sarajevo the siege.
When will it end?

Goradze

A wounded city
out in the open.
Obliterated from view
by poor communication.

The observer has retired
only the volunteers remain.
Easing the cities pain
from birth to oblivion.

World War CCC

World War III
has not turned out to be
the great conflagration
we expected it to be.

World War III
turned out to be
World War CCC.

Macedonia is a country again

Its official
Macedonia is a country again,
and to prove it
they've just beaten Liechtenstein 11-1.

The crowd will be going wild in the streets
of ehm, eh, ehm ......
Back to you in the studio Des.

Yesterday, Today and Tomorrow

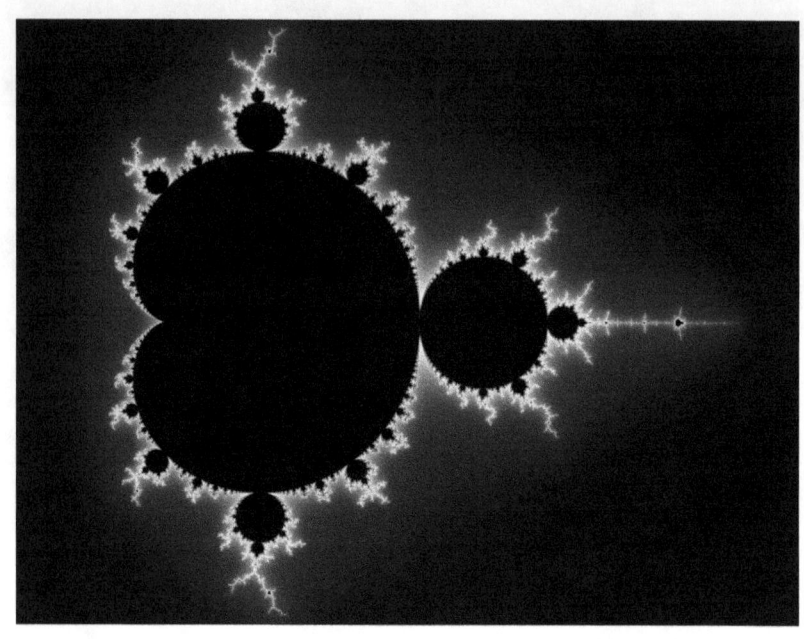

Barrings goes down

The Barrings butterfly.
A butterfly in far off Singapore.

A butterfly flaps his wings
in far off Singapore.
Flaps his wings
and the oldest bank is no more.

For Bao Ninh

Amidst the sorrow of war
I will see you here.

Wait for me here
after you have waited forever.

Amidst the sorrow of war
waiting will hurt no more.

Wait for me here
make me be here.

AKA The Chief Executive from Hell

I'm in charge of breaking the bad news
when its bad, when its news, its got to be me.

I'm in charge of breaking the bad news
when its good, when its news, its gotta be, someone else.

I'm in charge of breaking the bad news
when its simple, when its easy, it
              had better be
              mr.sleezy.
              [aka the chief executive from hell]

Amsterdam coffee shop

Watching over the children, who sit
aimlessly in small groups waiting.
Then the serious dealers appear waiting also.
The children keep rolling then the dealer
sits near and then so his friend.
They're rolling too but is it the same.
Let's see how they do this, this is their game.
No one is doing anything like thinking
everyone's playing their own game.
Sounds like it could be Morocco
who will play host to tonight's game.

That old refrain

Heading down to the clinic again
too many E's and speed again.

Heading down to be there again
another first night, wherever, again.

Heading down to the clinic again
expecting to hear much the same.

One more time with that old refrain
something perhaps, to ease the pain.

Maybe Einstein was wrong

What if Einstein was wrong
and we could travel faster than light (ftl).
A very early acronym for those collectors
of such interesting pieces of arcane linguistics.

Still, I digress,
what if Einstein was wrong.

Well,
how could it be done,
to fly us back in time.
Or should we just work on the assumption
that eventually some smart mathematician
will show us how it's done.
We are not mathematicians
so we assume one day it has been done.

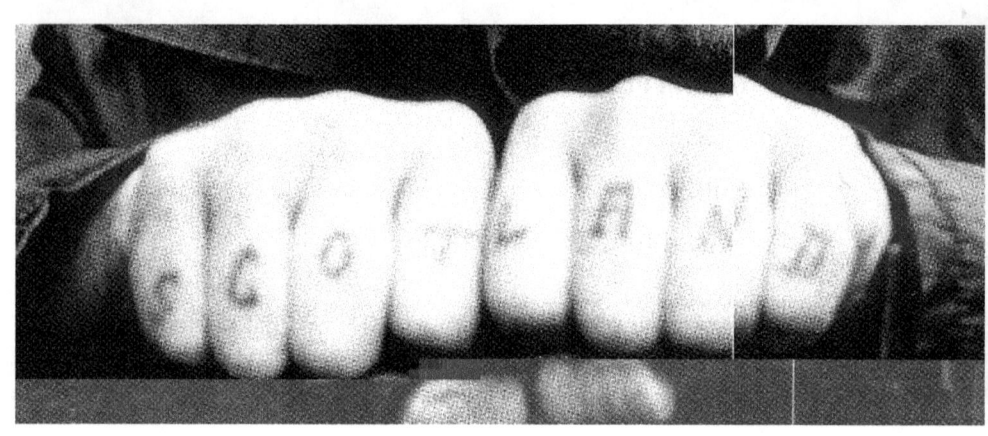

Tattoo Times

Tattoos in our times
the jewellery of the poor
paid for permanency
an expression as a jewel.

an expression of love
an expression of power
an expression of nationality
an expression of ownership
an expression of slavery

Tattoos of our times
a jewelled expression of emotion
proudly visible
to inflame and ignite.

After the plague

After the plague
there were few of us left,
rattling around in the empty cities.
Wondering, what now?

Everyone had gone.
Everyone left was searching again
for friends,
to begin again.

Holding Patterns

people in holding patterns
they make me uneasy
as they wait for the clock
      to turn.

people in holding patterns
they make me wary
as they wait to decide
      what next.

A Good Netizen?

I spoke face to face
with a stranger, for the first time
half way round the world
they were there, and I was here.

Face to face by wire
over the web, winding us together.
Hi doc he said
I replied it was my first time.

Face to face in chat
What sort of doc? Where from?
Wow my dads the same!
Thanks for the advice, got to go, bye.

Courier

Courier from culture to culture.
Courier of ideas to ideas.

The courier is the border
the courier is the mix
the courier is the new

sometimes flash
sometimes fame
sometimes forever

what courier to be
what courier to become.

A blank page to start
an idea to impart.
Don't listen, to that old *art.

more new neologisms

GIGADARK

Charged particles from the solar flare,
irradiate the infrastructure everywhere.

Charged particles from the solar flare,
lights out, lights out, everywhere.

www.gigadark.com

DATADUST

Accumulating detritus of the information age,
binary code and pixels in our wake.

Debris left behind in the machine,
binary code and pixels are our wake.

www.datadust.com

CHAOLIST

Do not do this when that happens,
do this when that does not happen.

When this happens do not do this,
if this does not happen, do this.

www.chaolist.com

CHAOLOGIST

An expert or student of chaos,
however improbable that may be.

Predicting everything unlikely to you and me,
however improbable that may be.

www.chaologist.com

ANTI-ORG

Where organisations fear to lead,
individuals change the world.

When organisations lead us astray,
you change the world.

www.anti-org.org

GIGAECHO

Some actions resonate beyond their limits,
returning changed in unimagined ways.

Every action ripples without limit,
spreading change in unanticipated ways.

www.gigaecho.com

colophon

This is my art

This is my art and this is me
what you get is what you see.

Don't ask me why this is me.

This is my art and this is me
what you see is what you get.

It's all of me and nothing yet.

'A sudden gust of wind at Ejiri' Katsushika Hokusai

*e*hold on

© PROHIBITED PUBLICATIONS
MMVIII

next

gluon notes

jamie inglis

© PROHIBITED PUBLICATIONS

MMVIII

www.prohibitedpublications.com

www.ingramcontent.com/pod-product-compliance
Lightning Source LLC
Chambersburg PA
CBHW071731040426
42446CB00011B/2310